Poetry Now - Poems From North & North West England 2005

Edited by Bobby Tobolik

First published in Great Britain in 2005 by:
Poetry Now
Remus House
Coltsfoot Drive
Peterborough
PE2 9JX
Telephone: 01733 898101
Website: www.forwardpress.co.uk

All Rights Reserved

© Copyright Contributors 2005

SB ISBN 1 84602 018 2

Foreword

Poetry Now was formed in 1989 with the aim of allowing struggling poets a much-needed opportunity to showcase their work in what is otherwise a very elitist industry. Since we launched our competition to discover the best of our regional poetry in the same year, it has always generated a huge amount of interest and proved continuously successful. 2005 marks our latest series of regional poetry, which we hope will be our best ever.

The poets in this collection draw inspiration from a wide variety of sources, including not only personal experience but also imagination and even historical fact. Not only are we able to share in the poet's own personal memories, but we can also enjoy the experience of discovering another's unique viewpoint on a number of issues.

The wide variety of styles and tones in this anthology means that there is something for everyone, and we hope you enjoy reading it as much as we enjoyed discovering afresh the best of our local poets.

Contents

Tracking	Abigail Markey	1
A Sonnet For Starr	Wendy Preece	2
The Knocker-Upper	Patricia B Spear	3
Evening Enchantment	Barbara Brannelly	4
Seashore Echo	Claire Newby	5
Ode To A Young Lady	Philip Snow	6
Pam	Wendy Seyben	7
To Pretty You	Mother Annabelle Preston	8
Epitaph For An Innocent	G R Bell	9
Desolation	Graham McNicol	10
Pattern Of Fear	Jane Looker	11
Every Time	Donald John Tye	12
The Dog	Ann Pickering	13
Frosty Morning	Greta Forsyth	14
Impressions Of Life	C R Slater	15
Immortalised In Black And White	Lilian Pickford-Miller	16
Coming Home	Ray Johnson	17
A Man Leans Over His Guitar, Writing	Doug Cairns	18
Tears	Chris Milburn	19
The Journey	Anne Marie Latham	20
Time Of Your Life	Jane Smailes	21
Nature's Balm	Kathleen Potter	22
On The Other Side	Alan C Brown	23
You Stole Him From Me	Vivienne C Wiggins	24
Holiday In France	Kenneth Mood	25
If I Could Send A Parcel	Alex Branthwaite	26
The Wind	Alan Adcock	27
Under The Rainbow	Rachel Lucinda Burns	28
True Connections	Angela Fothergill	29
Poetry Lane	Sara Newby	30
Emotions	Jessica Copland (14)	31
Anniversary	Aissatou Sylla	32
Surfacing . . .	David McConville	33
Poetry And Love	Gary Thompson	34
7/7	Sheila Wicks	35
Leather	Sara Campbell-Kelly	36
Marsden Moor	Heather Ferrier	37
My Mum	Debbie Davies	38

Wilmslow Road Manchester 2005	Irene Clare Garner	39
Asleep	Andy Beckett	40
A Dream	Mark Thirlwell	41
Beauty	H Dormand	42
Her Warning	Shadow Duffield	43
Shadows Of The Soul	Graham Connor	44
Human Race That's Ran	Christopher Newlove	45
Manannan	Valerie Caine	46
The Maypole Queen	James Stephen Cameron	47
My Liverpool	Ann McDermott	48
Forgotten World	Tommy McBride	49
The Countryside And Town	Rhian Parry (11)	50
The Countryside	John Parry	51
Endless Rain	Catherine Palin	52
Below Midnight	Peter Corbett	53
Janet	William Carr	54
Liverpool City Of Culture 2008	Eileen W O'Brien	55
Untitled	Atul Parab	56
Better Batter	Pat Ammundsen	57
Judgement	Abigail Flynn (13)	58
My Mum, Liverpool	Tom Roach	59
Mum	Kerry Hart	60
Chemistry	Robert Shorey	61
Oh, Mighty Lord	Debbie Storey	62
Untitled	Paul Barron	63
A Breath Of Fresh Air In Formby	Freda Grieve	64
The Broken House	A Wilkinson	65
Chapters	Sarah Jane Davies	66
My Hometown	Jeni Gidney	67
River Kent	Jack Edwards	68
With Me	Thomas Ian Graham	69
A Leaf In A Storm	Judy Rochester	70
Beautiful In Your Sadness	Katie Boyd	71
Confused? You Will Be	Jenny Messenger	72
Two Sights	Brian Frost	73
For Mam	Stephanie Williamson (8)	74
Requiem Of A Child	George Carrick	75
La Vida Es Una Perra	John Robinson	76
Belonging	Carolyn Smith	77
Global Warming	John Foster	78
Lakeland Fells	John R Parker	79

Cumbria	Jennifer H Fox	80
Immaculate Potential	Sam Dixon	81
It's Up To You/Sing For Justice	Margaret Ann Scott	82
A Tempestuous Night	J Parker	83
To Mother With Love	Jean Wood	84
My Countdown Dilemma	Christine Skeer	85
Changing Views	Sandra Roberts	86
Snowdrops At Rode Hall	Angela Pritchard	87
Childhood Refugee	Jennifer Hill	88
For The Love Of My Dad	Wendy Wilkinson	89
My Friend Teresa	Graham Bowers	90
The Cyclamen	Theresa M Carrier	91
Saint Nicholas	Esmond Simcock	92
By The Sea	C Rowley	93
A Stranger In The Street	Katie Cheetham	94
Bonnie Scotland	Phyllis Ing	95
Fear	Alice Higham	96
The Four Of Us	Nigel Astell	97
Padstow Born But No Bread	Ian Jobson	98
Liverpool, My Liverpool	Joan Harris	99
Transparent Peace	Hilary Jean Clark	100
Unamused	William Anthony Ralphson	101
The Vision	Bill Austin	102
Angels	Carolina de la Cruz	103
Ash Tree In My Hedge	Mary Hodges	104
My Family Tied Down	Claire Smith	105
Death Of The King	Brian Croft	106
Salt Of The Earth	Glenda Stryker	107
Happy Motoring In The North West	Tim Hoare	108
Pathway Of Life	Susan Carr	109
Awaiting Death	Christopher Kennedy	110
The Netherwoods	Joyce Graham	111
The Tall Men	Raymond Pilling	112
A Rare Gift	Yasmeen Ahmed	113
Inspiration	E Riverside	114
Cracked Rainbows	David Charles	115
July	Hayes Turner	116
Changing Tides	Margaret Parnell	117
The Written Word	Ellen Spiring	118
Lament	Paul Anthony Scott	119
Spring	Simon Kilshaw	120

My Church	Margaret B Baguley	121
Someone To Care	Linda Howitt	122
Metamorphosis	Lesley J Worrall	123
Out Of Sight	Chris Creedon	124
Ode To Black Pudding Chucking	Philip Corbishley	125
Untitled	Catherine Hunter	126
A Personal Forfeit!	M Ross	127
For All Eternity	Jim Thomas	128
Little Alien	Kevin Baskin	129
Thorns	Adrian Salamon	130

The Poems

Tracking

I was born facing desert heat
from father
wasteland sand
and crags of mother
I learnt to read late but long
before, I taught myself sign
and kept walking in this strange
place
lost -
terror passed for courage
one foot pushing forward
in front of the other
and in the midst of it all
realised I was surviving
and then wondered why . . .

I looked back to
nothing familiar
I lay on the earth watching
it heal, wishing too
that mine could be healed
so I went back
to the point last seen
the point before I was lost
and started to walk alongside myself
facing memories and fears
the end of hope
accepting there's no way home
learning to see the bad and the good
wishing for a happy ending
thinking if I concentrate on the good
it'll diminish the bad,
but it doesn't work
so I continue walking
establish a stride
walking alongside myself
in this cold landscape known as truth.

Abigail Markey

A Sonnet For Starr

Starr is my rocking horse, made long ago;
He's older than my grandpa and my nan.
Some say he's Victorian - I don't know,
Maybe he was here when the world began!

We'd go on such adventures, Starr and I;
We'd gallop over mountains wild and free.
I'd climb upon his back - and off we'd fly,
Or very gently canter by the sea.

I'm quite old and worn now, and so is he;
His mane and tail are very nearly gone.
The years of toil show - for all to see,
Yet this dapple-grey is loved by everyone.

His eyes are still bright, and his smile so wide,
He'd dearly love to take you for a ride!

Wendy Preece

The Knocker-Upper

Gas lamps
casting light in the fog.
Spooky . . .
A shadowy figure,
holding aloft
a long pole
with spokes at the top.
Then
Rat-a-tat-tat, rat-a-tat-tat
at the bedroom window.
Rat-a-tat-tat
repeated.
It is six in the morning . . .
time to awake.

A light,
in the room above him.
Sleepy face
behind curtains.
the wave of a hand.
His job is done.
He moves on.

His reign
over the silence,
soon to be disturbed
by the tramping
of clogs
along cobbled streets.
In their hundreds,
workers
head for the pits
or the weaving sheds . . .
where they'll begin
their working day.

Patricia B Spear

Evening Enchantment

Not a soul did mar the beauty, of that evening long ago.
Shadows long, transformed the landscape
Revealing mysteries no one knows

Knights ride high on swirling waters
Damsels at the castle walls
Gulls wailing as if remembering
When men came to fight the foe.

But no memories can spoil this beauty
Of a sun's red, silken folds
Sinking swiftly in the distance
Magnificent in its earthly roll.

Seagulls swoop in wild abandon
Screeching their long and eerie cry.
But just as one is lost in its beauty
A blanket of grey unfolds in the sky.

Peace descends as the day is lost,
Never to return again.
I feel your arms enclose my body
You hold me close, I kiss your lips
The wind blows cold in ghostly whispers
As we melt into the misty night.

Barbara Brannelly

Seashore Echo

Time dictates the world, here it is lost,
I lay in the grass, Man's Heaven looks down,
the sky starts blue, few clouds interrupting,
blue turns to orange, red dances above,
Beach below cliffs, swallowed by the sea,
God streaks the sky with pinks, subtle purple,
I sit, I wrap my arms around myself,
gentle winds caress me, I'm shivering,
the sun starts to drown, the sea is waiting,
darkness has captured me, night commences,
I will give you up, the grasshoppers play,
I will crave you, the wind whistles for me,
I will return next summer, wind whistles,
I love you it repeats, I love you too.

Claire Newby

Ode To A Young Lady

I walked with her
On that November afternoon
In the autumn of her youth,
And saw her once again, as it were,
For the first time
As, mirrored in those golden tints
She recounted tales of yesterday,
With lucid, bitter longing.
Like the trees was she,
Wistful in the memories of fleeting seasons
Forgiving time and days so swiftly passed,
Accepting everything that came and went so quickly,
Quiet and satisfied with the harvest of her youth.
And in that quietness, of yesterdays remembered,
I saw tomorrow slumbering,
A quiet flame, abiding in the depths of her,
As spring abides the passing of the coldest winter days,
Ready to burn again in the fullness of another season.
And as I looked at her I saw that slumbering tomorrow
Accept the glories and pains of all her yesterdays
To live with joy together,
That every passing year may be enriched,
Gathering into one the fruits of nature's patient growth and harvest
That as tomorrow newly dawns, wholeness into wholeness
                                                  may increase

And bliss be born again.
It was as if I saw the whole of life in her,
As I walked with her,
On that November day.

Philip Snow

Pam

Pam will be sixty soon,
Born just after the war, a baby boom.
Tall and slim, a blonde bombshell,
She doesn't look sixty, you'd never tell.
Always dresses very smart,
When she goes out, she looks the part.

She's not a happy bunny,
Being sixty isn't funny.
Necks go saggy,
Eyes go baggy,
Mouths droop,
Backs stoop,
Utter nonsense, it's not true,
It won't apply to you.

On your birthday, you'll be glad
Of all the wonderful times you've had.
You've got a trade in your fingers,
Your skills are sublime
Accept being sixty and have a good time.

Put on your glad rags and hit the town,
Paint it red; don't wear a frown,
Don't tell anyone you're sixty,
They won't believe you; they'll stare in disbelief
Because like me - you're twenty-one underneath.

Wendy Seyben

To Pretty You

Pretty you,
Pretty in your heart
Because you are kind,
We love you.

Although you don't
See us and we
Don't see you,

We do see you,
In a way,
With our prayer,
And our hope is
There, for you
To be happy.

We hope you, our flower,
Hope you grow
And you know
We always do
Love you.

Mother Annabelle Preston

Epitaph For An Innocent

Weep not for Pamela Lynn.
Her life the merest speck upon the sands of time,
who for the few days that she lived
knew only of the safety of a mother's love.
Weep not for Pamela Lynn, victim of the hypocrites
who masquerade as saviours of their fellow men,
but, crazed with greed and lust for power,
send their sadist butchers in
to slaughter without mercy or remorse
the gentlefolk who pose no threat to anyone.
Weep for the world
that spawns these murderous men.
But grieve for Pamela Lynn.

G R Bell

Desolation

From the night
Came the dawn,
Another boy was born
To a mother
Who couldn't feed
The child at her knee.

See the light,
Look at the light,
It blesses you
You'll be all right,
I hope you have
A better life than me,
It's too painful to pray.

Goodbye, goodbye little boy,
And with pain locked away,
She didn't stay,
She walked away,
She walked away,
She walked away.

Graham McNicol

Pattern Of Fear

Come! my little child, jump from the cliff,
Father is waiting, arms open, 'Come live!'
Pattern of fear, none as a child
Gleefully sprawling by Father's side.

Come my young girl, take hold of my hand,
Through wooded lanes and bridle land.
Patter of fear, still none as a girl,
Thus happily wandered, head in a whirl.

Come my sweet woman, fall in love with me,
Your lips are for kissing, you're meant to be free.
Pattern of fear rose its ugly head
And soon I found I was in his bed.

Come my duly wife, do all that I say,
The baby is crying, and meals are delayed.
Pattern of fear now strong and bold,
So tired of rows, the drink takes hold.

Come my dear patient, we will make you well,
Wine and drowning are not your kind of hell.
Pattern of fear, slowly goes away,
Head filled with a new life, I'll start today.

Come graceful lady, let's walk in the park,
Your life's passing by - old, wise, soon to embark
On a new life, away from patterns of fear,
Your soul says goodbye to you, your death so near.

Come all you mourners, tears are a waste,
This woman lived well, all to her taste.
The pattern of fear which caused her doom,
Now laid to rest with her, and her tomb.

Jane Looker

Every Time

Every time I look into
Your hazel-brown eyes,
My very thankful heart
Takes a grateful sigh
For I know I'm holding tenderly
In my arms
An angel from Heaven above
An angel of beauty
I will always love
With the whole of my heart
And soul
For she is the angel in my life
She is my warm and tender
Sweet, loving wife
And her angel's name is Gillian Rose
Sweet Gillian Rose Gwinnette.

Donald John Tye

The Dog

The iron bars a barrier form,
To gaze upon the outside world
With sad anticipation.

While up and down the street,
His leaping eyes are searching now,
Across the busy road.

From early morn with ears alert
And hopeful gaze at those who pass,
He keeps a tireless vigil.

What pleasures he has planned,
To greet the long delayed return
Of his beloved master.

In favours great, there is but one
And he has journeyed far away
To another life.

With pleading eyes of velvet brown,
He asks the question once again,
'Where is he now?'

Ann Pickering

Frosty Morning

Green-white is the earth today
caught up in winter's frosty spray
Mottled silver-brown fingers of trees
shake and sway in the morning breeze
The surging white spumes of angry seas
violently crash onshore, wild and free
Trampling footfall hard under heel
Hard, crispy, stiff and crunchy the feel
Glistening glints, sparkled all around
field upon field of ice-cold ground
Imprinted trails of walkers long passed
scarred the soil of winter looking glass

Greta Forsyth

Impressions Of Life

With age, life's faster, and years, they rush past,
And days seem to pass by, ever more so, so fast.
With each day in life, we're always leaving behind
Little footprints of ourselves in other folks' minds.
We should guard actions wisely, not cuss or swear,
Leave an imprint of ourself, with no dishonour there,
Instead we leave weary hearts behind, day after day,
Rather than leaving sunshine, and smiles, all the way.
We should be remembered with smiles and laughter,
In the many hearts of those we love, forever and after.
For when we pass on, it's best done without any pain,
Of turning in your grave from a past life's sad reign.
We should leave behind a lifetime's work of fine art,
That shows we were considerate, for others, at heart.
Maybe then we can smile down from Heaven above,
Filling the air with serene, angelic, radiant love.
We would get pats on the back from the angels up high,
As without malice or hate, our name's surely held high.
Guard actions and words wisely, curb thought and tongue
Leave a light within others through the path you will run.

C R Slater

Immortalised In Black And White

How beautiful it was back then
in the days when I was a child
now the scenery only exists
in pictures in my mind
and a handful of photographs
that have been immortalised in black and white.
Two schools and streets of houses
now take the place
of where natural lakes once used to be
how prosperous would be now
our little town of Hebburn
if the lakes still existed for all to enjoy and see
but all we have left to pass on to our children
are our recalled memories and a handful of photographs
immortalised in black and white.

Lilian Pickford-Miller

Coming Home

I've been away on holiday
Although the place was fine
It will never ever replace
The views along the Tyne

The people are so friendly
And will pass the time o' day
There's Geordies and Mackems
And folks from Whitley Bay

So the wise men in the councils
Then called it Tyne and Wear
There's castles and there's churches
And stadiums to shout and cheer

There are green hills all around us
A vision for all to share
Coming home is so wonderful
I'm proud that I live there

Visitors to this region
Some come with open mind
Then leave chock full of memories
Of places, and the people left behind

The vision of the bridges
Or the Angel of the North
A glimpse of Penshaw monument
An invitation to come forth

Some complain about the weather
Now! we are generous there
Come rain, hail or sunshine
You will always get your share.

Ray Johnson

A Man Leans Over His Guitar, Writing

Like the story-teller
Turned songwriter
Who with simple phrases
And magic that is by nature practised and accidental
Brings a picture to mind
That shakes your thoughts
And hurts your heart
By no fault of your own

Doug Cairns

Tears

How you must have cried with that farewell hug and kiss.
Trying to cement the memories,
The touch of the skin,
The look in the eyes,
The intoxication of smells,
Is it auf wiedersehen or goodbye?

Not a day went by without a thought of me.
The hope and belief that I'd be happy was a balance to
The sadness, noticeable at times to those closest to you,
But never explained until mortality approached.

How you must smile now, seeing me as part of the
Family, the jigsaw complete.

No bitterness, there never was,
Just unity and tears of joy.

Chris Milburn

The Journey

As I puff and pant on the road to work,
Sights and noises abound,
Raucous mooing and a distant neigh,
'Good morning to you too,' I say.

As far as the horizon, all is green,
A patchwork of emerald beauty,
And up above, all is blue,
A cloud-dappled, sapphire expanse.

Powerful hums draw the eyes to the sky,
Jet-filled planes, soaring laden-full,
Carrying passengers to a destiny unknown,
A link to the wider world.

And are there many people to view this wonder?
Not many, in fact very few,
But plenty of cars hurtle down the road,
Faster and faster and faster.

A beautiful way to lower your cholesterol,
Plenty of pound-shedding hills,
But I could do with a pub halfway round,
Sugar-free and diet-friendly.

A bracing start and finish to the day,
A freedom in which to breathe,
And would we swap this for warmer climes?
'Why no, man! We love Britain's chilly North-East.'

Be grateful you have such beauty to enjoy.
And don't forget to thank Him,
For the hand that crafted this gift of nature,
Lives here, in this heavenly oasis.

Anne Marie Latham

Time Of Your Life

Arrival time, opening time,
Wait time, waste time,
Pass time, past time,
Play for time, do time,
Bad times, good times,
Old times in no time,
Beat time, two-time,
Old Tyme waltz time,
Time off, part-time,
Time out, half-time,
Father Time, extra time,
Time has come,
It's full time

Jane Smailes

Nature's Balm

Through warped wooden door creaking with age
A glimpse of creation's noble stage
Rioting greens, a hundred varied shades
Meandering paths dip through leafy glades
Protected from seasons' moods capricious
Bees drone a lullaby - time ceases
Sun's baby-soft hand stroke haloed ground
Saluting charms of glory uncrowned,
Gift-wrapped balm, solitude and silence.

Geordie idiom shatters sad reverie
'Yon grey lap tails survive adversity
Even in our blustering north-easterlies
Nesting here for nigh on two centuries.
Aye, life's awful strange with no guarantees'
From grief's miasma a soul he frees
Angst and pipe smoke slow, mingling, rising
In late heat an ancient soliloquising.
Provocation or illumination?

Seats' slats empty, peaked cap venerable gone
Caught in atmosphere his words linger on
Igniting a tiny flame to nurture
Tremulous bud of hope for the future
Pungent wild garlic assails the nostrils
Brave violets poke through ivy's tendrils
Remembrance stripped of its hurtful powers
Leaves a heart space to savour the flowers.
While contemplating and appreciating.

Kathleen Potter

On The Other Side
(To Gertrude Bell 1868 - 1926)

I am the first to walk into the window of your name
others saw shuttered, blank. Though you are dead
you're breathing yet where small leaves come into touch.
Look! It's for you the sun's disk bleeds at dusk;
for you infolded sand whispers: *Sleep, sleep!*
billowing round your hair without admittance.
Your hair is an ashen house, a threadbare moon;
looking up I enter its crinkled moist smell.
Among silenced strangers I alone can sing
the dropped brown bird of your voice. You are she
who carries the stopped clock of my worst hour
gently under one arm, refusing to throw
it away. For that I am grateful. You are she
who veins my hands, as sand grains vein basalt rock,
as the sky's veined with stars at beneficent daybreak.

How else can your kind come back unless someone
stepping indoors drinks the wind's grave; spiralling stars;
mirage on the horizon shaped like your heart?
Look! I am he who drinks your travelling footprints,
one after one, Gertrude, until like wind-blown sand
gradually succeeds in closing deep gaps in it.
I alone smooth your bruised eyes into a smile.
Two nights, two closed red roses splash your face
with the soft perfumed fragrance of Hafiz.
Ah! Among women where is your equal? Can one
such as you come back among us? We think not.
Searching a crinkled sea of women's featureless
cold faces near dawn we ask, *'In whom now can
we drink dreams since your bright wheel has stopped?'*

Alan C Brown

You Stole Him From Me

Flutter her lashes
Flash those long legs
Coy girly giggle
'Just once more!' she begs
He is over the moon
And under her thumb
He's lost common sense
And has been struck dumb
She's all that he talks about
I'm out of the scene
When there's new blood around
Who wants a has-been?

Yes, you stole him from me
In that innocent way you do
How can you know so much
. . . When you're only two?

Vivienne C Wiggins

Holiday In France

Making two sandcastles
with my younger sister.
Putting white feathers in the top.
The concentration of the action
is incredible.

The beach is nearly empty
like sand in a blue glass.
My hair is wet and my shadow
is like an elephant.

Kenneth Mood

If I Could Send A Parcel

If I could send a parcel
to Africa far away -
it would hold a magic rubber
to erase their debts away.

This parcel would have a water tap
refreshing and sparkling clean,
water holes would be obsolete
and sterile soil made green.

This parcel would have medicines
to help all of those in need
children would be vaccinated
and given proper feed.

The parcel is mythical
a fresh die has been set
'Live 8' is a reality -
to clear the African debt.

Alex Branthwaite

The Wind

I love the sound the wind makes when it whistles through the trees,
The eerie light a fire gives when fanned by blowing breeze,
It's almost always thereabouts, yet we can't see its face,
Sometimes it blows with all its force as though 'twere in a race.

I love the feeling that it gives when rippling o'er your skin,
Then swiftly it accelerates and makes a mighty din,
Rattling doors around the house and buckles the windowpane,
It tests and looks for weaknesses, it's then it is insane.

The wind's a necessity that drives the daily weather,
If something's loose outside the house, better that you tether,
Or it may fly across the ground and take an unknown ride,
And who knows where or when it falls upright or on its side.

I hate the way it drives the hail and hurls it in your face,
Better that you go inside, till it slows its frenzied pace.
When winter comes and snow arrives and lies upon the ground,
The gusting winds will whip it up and pile it all around.

It is our friend for all of that, creating power too,
By driving round the windmill's arms, it's an electric coup,
Fresh ways will constantly be sought, for free wind power, new,
I know this force, will always be; and what a good job too.

Alan Adcock

Under The Rainbow

Under the rainbow a sculpture,
Spreads its wings across Tyneside.
Burnt rust-red, a vulture,
Its beady eye watches the northern sky.

Standing still, a bloody thumb in the horizon.
Ninety thousand every day gaze on its bronzed side.
The local residents expressed their doubts at its arrival.
'How much?' they asked. 'We don't care if it's an icon.'

They weren't interested in the facts,
That it would beautify in time over the River Tyne,
That its wingspan was wider than a jumbo jet,
That it would attract visitors from far and wide.

Do the local people feel differently now?
Have they learnt to love the bronzed angel in their midst,
Or do they still begrudge the lump of rusty metal?
Do they still persist to grumble, why?

The Angel of the North, spread its wings,
A crock of gold under the rainbow,
And over the rainbow a bird sings,
The money spent could have been put to better things.

Rachel Lucinda Burns

True Connections

The connection had been cut
And ever since then you would wonder
If we could ever feel it again.

I would struggle, as did you,
And when the time came
A million wishes and dreams
Had just come true.

Older now, I feel the same.

However, I have my own connections
Blossoming, as I also feel the struggle.
Hoping myself and my own will feel it again.

I will ease their drear cries
Until like us dear Mother
We must only say, 'Goodbye.'

Angela Fothergill

Poetry Lane

A narrow road leading nowhere
I call it Poetry Lane
Whenever I walked down there
Inspiration always came.

There's nothing very much to see
Some trees, some fields, a farm.
A stream that flows under a bridge
I sit there when it's warm.

I sit and write some poetry
About birds that sing in the trees
And I try to recapture the feeling
Of a warm, summer breeze.

I've written about the splendour
Of a colourful autumn day
And even fog and cloudy skies
In November, cold and grey.

I've tried to describe December
With snow and sleet and rain
Inspiration never fails me
When I stroll down Poetry Lane.

Sara Newby

Emotions

I need to know what's right for me
I have to find a key
Or all my heart desires
Will be locked inside of me

What do I have to look for?
What do I have to find?
All I know is that I must
Look throughout my mind

Love is so important
So when you fall in deep
Throughout our heart's content
It's the end that makes us weep

If it tingles in your fingers
Or even in your toes
What will hate feel like?
I hope I'll never know

So next time you think you've
Found your one true love
Lift your head and look up
And read the stars above

Jessica Copland (14)

Anniversary

Dear X,
Because your demise is not even worth celebrating,
I am just reiterating your death
Y has taken your place in my life,
Followed by Z, then A, B, C and D.

See how dead you are.
You're so dead that I can no longer remember
Your face, your eyes, your smile,
Your voice, whispers and breath
Your smell, your touch, *your punch.*

Dear and buried, you are!
You've had right
To funerary rites
So may you rest in peace
Please rest in peace
And leave me in peace
Instead of infecting my betraying dreams.

Aissatou Sylla

Surfacing . . .

Breaking dark water,
Breathing the salt into the air;
Floating on an ocean
Of white light.

Drifting on a wave of azure.
Sleeping, gently sleeping

Knowing, always knowing

I would finally surface . . .

David McConville

Poetry And Love

I am going to write poetry until the day I die,
I want to thrill you all before the day I die,
To entertain that's what I believe I'm here for,
Until the day I die I'm yours so don't let go, I love you so!

Pure poetry, I could write about you, the love we have,
I could write about how wonderful the world is,
How pretty it all is, how glad I am to be alive,
How glorious it all is, my dream paradise, I love you all,

Creativity springs from me, creating harmony, peace
                                            and understanding,
Let's create passion, passion between me and you, a rose
                                                    can say it all,
Dreaming, let's dream together, it seems like Alice springing
                                          into God's wonderful world,
Beautiful, it's all so beautiful.

I love you so, I need you so,
Never leave me, never go, I'm so in love with you,
Poetry and love, let's write together, from the day we met to
        the day we part, as long as we know if you're not there
                                                  how can I breathe?
Poetry and love, let's end this poem now until the next one,
Yet again we'll meet.

Gary Thompson

7/7

Morning; sit on the garden swing.
Peace, beauty, tranquillity.
Morning; standing room only on the tube.
Another dull day at the office.

Distant traffic, a far-off bark.
Birds, competing to keep the silence at bay.
Blasting, gut ripping, mind shrieking roar,
Primeval screams, sobs, profanities and prayers.

Multicoloured flowers unfurling in the early sunshine.
Dew drying on the green velvet grass.
Seething, swirling, dirt and dust
Bright red blood pouring onto the torn tangled wreckage.

The gentle touch of moving air,
The tickle of a tiny insect.
The shocking pain of tearing tissue.
The bubbling burning of scorched skin.

The fragrance of the flowers
And aroma of herbs soothe the soul.
Noisome, evacuated bowels, burnt flesh,
Poisonous fumes all gag the mind.

The coffee tasted good, I rise from the swing
Refreshed, ready to start the day.
The dirty air tasted of choking death
Those who could, crawled towards life.

Sheila Wicks

Leather

Leather sweat,
Hot and tight.
We're escaping from real life tonight.

My skin,
The only thing
Keeping
Me
From
Being
Everywhere
All at once;
Is soaking you in.
Remembering,
Savouring.

Drinking up the smell of you,
Thirstily,
Readily.
Darkness stops time,
To make you mine
For a while.

And as our hearts
Drip, waxed love
Onto hot promises,
The polka-dot flames rise.

Sara Campbell-Kelly

Marsden Moor

In an outbreak of exuberance
that peppery prankster wind rushed clowning;
playfully twirled the tea from our cups,
whisked a lettuce leaf from my sandwich,
sent it bouncing across the tussocks.
We listened to the husky rustling
in a sea of browns and buffs
amid the slowly rolling waves
of last year's wind dried grass.

In an upsurge of lightheartedness
frolicsome gusts ran billowing up
from over the hill, galloping astride,
to pluck the winter dried dead blades
and deliver them to be arrayed
on a simple two strand barbed wire fence.
Quite loaded up, festooned and swagged
like a troupe decked out in skirts of grass,
they shimmied and shook in lively dance.

Heather Ferrier

My Mum

There's someone I know who's always been there, loving and
kind with hugs to spare.
She's helped me through times, good and bad, wiped my
tears when I've been sad.
Helped me grow up to know wrong from right, always been there
for me day and night.
There's nothing too much trouble for this helper of mine, she's always
on hand, time after time.
She's taught me to love, to be kind and to treasure the family ties that
are too great to measure.
Without a doubt she cares for me, her love and kindness
shine for all to see.
She listens and helps without a complaint, she never gets tired of me -
she's a total saint.
There's no question about it - she's the best ever. *My mum*, my star,
my best friend for ever.
Her beauty, her kindness, her time and her love are all special gifts
she received from above.
She kept them inside her and then passed them on to make sure that
life's goodness would never be gone.
And time is now racing who knows what's to be. But I know that I've
no regrets about my mum and me.
We've been happy forever; our love is so strong and I know
in her arms, I will always belong.
I hope that one day my daughters will see that I'm a good mum -
like mine is to me.
And that they will pass on - as I have to them how to love and to care
for your children, Amen.
It's a pity that more people are not like my mum and cherish their
children forever to come.
Cos I know if they were this world would be great *my mum*,
my best friend, my world and my mate.

Debbie Davies

Wilmslow Road Manchester 2005

The buses are taken over by students
Already

A man with one leg got on
Struggling with his crutches
Only nobody got up for him
He tossed and fell about
With every rattle
Every brake.

I got off
On Portland Street
Went for
A twenty minute swim
No one else in the pool
Someone had left the water running
In the shower
Another was spread
The full length
Of the hair dryer bar
Shoes - make-up - bags - hair straightener
        and her towel
        at the far end
I moved it
The towel
She gave me a look to kill!

Irene Clare Garner

Asleep

All those words left unsaid,
The depression in the pillow where you laid your head,
Your clothes lined up, your shoes collecting dust
You slid away without any fuss.

You ceased to be my darling one,
Breathless you lay,
Asleep you seemed,
But the stillness was too much
I know you could never feel my touch.

As time invades this moment I lose you again,
Small memories, your sweet scent, the sound of your voice,
Become lost in this void.
Nothing will replace what you meant to me,
My sweet darling, who swapped pain, for eternity.

Andy Beckett

A Dream

My bed made
Doldrum smooth
Viridescence washed
Its feathered shore

Mark Thirlwell

Beauty

Models glide elegantly down the catwalk
Giving their designer smiles
Young girls watch them and think
I will be as thin as them in a little while.

Diets are not to be taken lightly
They might help reduce the pounds
But when the diet is stopped
The pounds again come around.

Some may not be pretty
But have voluptuaries' figures, to women's chagrin
And when they walk down the street
Men's eyes follow them, as we have seen.

Other people have luxurious hair
But sit in wheelchairs, they could be hiding their grief
While some can dazzle you with a smile
Showing a mouthful of white teeth.

One may have a sunny disposition, making everyone smile
But they could be deprived of love and affection
Their smile gaining them attention,
Could be just for a short while.

Beautiful eyes are a bonus
This person could be here, but in another land
Their minds could be troubled
With thoughts we wouldn't understand.

So remember there is always beauty
Even if it is difficult to find
You just have to take your time looking
Yes, it is there to see, if you insist on not being blind.

H Dormand

Her Warning

Draped within an evolution of society,
Cloaked by the sanity around all that lives,
Every breath of oxygen drawn is wasted upon words of cruelty,
So much hatred possessed in the emotions of actions,
Anguish and punishment is destined for our future,
Engraved in the eyes and scarred in the mind is all that has past,
Souls have shattered, like that of the fallen pane,
Tomorrow has been forgotten before yesterday has endeavoured,
Each day is numbered, the hourglass constantly eroding,
Out of control are the distinctions of acceptance,
Acceptance bound for all humanity,
Our nation's survival depends on our outlook of sudden change,
Today is the day when we must alter our urges of indulgent,
Nature's warnings have been invoked across the world,
Listen to her everyday sounds and watch in awe,
Watch the destruction she can create,
She holds a power so strong that mankind could never defeat,
Her temperament is raising,
Our transformations are but only bleak,
She has warned with decisive precision to make change,
Today this change is instructed to happen,
Tomorrow may never arise.

Shadow Duffield

Shadows Of The Soul

In the shadows lay the reflection of the soul
As we wander the world in a search to be whole
And we face the demons that made us once run away
Become friendly faces at the end of the day
Yet where does the day lie in-between?
The Lord himself divides the screen
Repose the day within my heart
That saw my dreams torn apart
I search for hope but yet the pain
Left but yet returns again
Yet life shall bring a melody
Of what we were and used to be
Images itself, me and my friend
Brings this story to an end.

Graham Connor

Human Race That's Ran

Time dies as I put the news on
It says it's the end of the week
But I know they'll be a new one
This is the human race that's ran.

The time of my life will be mine
I work to live and nothing else
Go home still I await my free time
This is the human race that's ran.

I've nothing to lose but my mind
I spend time like money on sh*t
I've lost the pieces of my pride
This is the human race that's ran.

I'm down, my time's up, I feel pain
I have just made the rich richer
And my offspring will do the same
We are the human race that's ran.

Christopher Newlove

Manannan

Manannan Mac Lir treads softly within his own cloak
Draped protectively about his adopted home.
Drawing it closer to his mighty breast
He seeks solace within its darkness.
Raiders withdraw in confusion,
Thoughts of plunder erased from their minds as
Their vessels become trapped with Manannan's magic web.
He sits within his labyrinth weaving stories and incantations
As they circumnavigate.
A momentary glimpse ignites their longing,
But the necromancer casts his spell
And the island melts away.
Wayfarers are deluded by the sight of a thousand men,
Deceived by a fleet of supernatural ships
And retreat.

Valerie Caine

The Maypole Queen

As she dances on thin vapour air,
Below woolly white clouds,
The maypole queen is seen,
With the freshness of early spring.

With innocence and childlike laughter,
Through green summertime meadows,
And silver gossamer threads,
Which hang dreamlike in suspension,

Old merry England,
With dreamy surreal days,
Where hide crickets and grasshoppers,
Through the dapple of sunlight,

Whilst kissing the soft breeze,
A beautiful summer vista opens,
And I shall kiss the purple heather of the Mann,
This savage, wild, uncontrollable beauty,

Below polished colossal stars,
Beside a treacherous foreboding sea,
The maypole queen is seen lovingly,
Whilst picking wild fruit and flowers,

With a declaration of love and beauty,
Her heart of fragrance and scents,
Whilst reading love poems and muse,
She dances wildly in trance with nature.

Besides the sweet bowers of paradise,
Where a million sunflowers sway on a gentle breeze,
And fairies and creatures cultivate invisibly,
Where the maypole queen has been,

Exploring a bright enchanted world,
Where God has worked spiritually,
With beautiful dreamlike miracles,
For mankind and beast alike.

James Stephen Cameron

My Liverpool

She's brash
She's funny
She's in your face
She's music
She's dance
She's on your case
She's comedy
She's tragedy
She's played many parts
She's writers
She's comics
She's first in the arts
She's beauty
She's grot
She's been well tested
She's proms
She's the river
She's never been bested
She's fashion
She's passion
She'll never walk alone
She's Goodison
She's Anfield
She's elation and groan
She's worship
She's unis
She get top marks
She's Cathedrals
She's cafes
She's larks in the parks
She's ferries
She's the 'Phil'
She's forever witty
She's friendly
She's proud
She's the world in one city.

Ann McDermott

Forgotten World

I envisaged a ferocious, relentless rainforest fire that
        was escalating, way out of control.
A small magnifying lens, that had been left behind carelessly,
        simply ignited the large Amazon Bowl.
I could smell mahogany embers of tall trees being scorched,
        that alopeciad the lush Brazilian terrain.
There were cultures, villages, whole generations wiped
        out, I perceived flames, yet my face felt rain.

Heart touched deeply; raw emotions ran reckless, by the
        Capitalists making vast fortunes from wood.
Those unsuspecting, disadvantaged Third World poor were left
abandoned and homeless in the mud.
I caught sight of an Indian tribesman who was scarred,
his burnt hands cupping water to singed lips.
He was carrying his means for his very next meal, a
simple blow-pipe with the darts of poisoned tips.

Tasting black water flavoured by ash, quenching his thirst
amidst the billowing smoke.
He was coughing up sputum that was stained tarry black,
gasping; sadly starting to choke.
Trapped animal screams deafening to my ears,
I smelt aromas of their raw, roasted skin.
Pandemonium had arrived in the disappearing world, amidst
the clattering, clamorous din.

Hark the Herald Angels are now silent; I no longer
        hear their sweet songs.
All that these destitute people had held sacred once,
        have absolutely nowhere now to belong.
There was haunting sounds from a hopeful Jesuit's flute, shredding
sorrow through the ballads he played.
Down on both knees, facing the Heavens above, Bible clenched in his
hands as he prayed.

His cloth habit had fungus, which was forming from the mildew.
His eyes scanning columns, as if it were a cathedral nave.
Praying desperately to his God for those unfortunate people,
pleading if they and their sacred land could be saved?

Tommy McBride

The Countryside And Town

Millions of daisies,
I see no grass;
Trees surrounding me.
But I see some light,
Peeking through branches and leaves;
Dark colours like green and brown,
Apart from daisies.

Millions of houses,
I see no plants;
Walls, bricks, around me.
But I see a patch of grass,
In-between a church and a house;
Man-made things, not changed at all,
Apart from houses.

Millions of stones,
On road and by river;
Some black, grey, in-between.
For they remind us of memories,
Good and bad, happy or sad.
They also tell us things in their own way,
Like countryside or town.

Rhian Parry (11)

The Countryside

I set out into the freshness of the morning,
The warmth of the sun on my face.
What better than a walk in the countryside.
The morning air fills my lungs.
The scent of the flowers intoxicates me.
Sways of golden corn gently roll in the fields.
Along the streams, songbirds sing their songs of love.
How I love the countryside.
To see young lambs leaping for joy,
Their mother gently grazing on the hillside,
Can anybody not like the beauty of this?

John Parry

Endless Rain

As I see you laying there, eyes looking back
Through a bottomless stare
I wish that there were more I could do
Just to let you know I care for you
I place my hand upon your own
As I force a smile of hope and pray
You may live to see another day
Fighting back an army of tears
As I brush away hair from behind those ears
Leaning in toward your frozen frame, I whisper,
'Say those sacred words to me,
The final breath to come from thee'
I cannot move, nor blink an eye
Yet I still can sense your hurt inside
Like an endless rain you cry
You care deeply for me, I see it now
In a dreamlike state, as I wonder how
And why, you have to deal with this pain
I can feel your love as you pray for me
You'll have my last breath, the way it should be
With one final leap of faith
One last burst of strength, forgiving all
This is my final curtain call
Squeezing your hand in mine
Before the deciding cut on my lifeline
As I whisper those final words
My arm you touch, as you hold my limp body close
I love you so much.

Catherine Palin

Below Midnight

Mesmerising in the hallowed light
The pin pricks of Heaven
Stare forever
Behind deep black velvet
Curtain walls;
Where the Nut womb calls
For us to follow
Catching the answers
In a bird's flight
To a new tomorrow.

There the cool cocoon
Of your body
Meshed in silk wires
Ties me to your truth
A fragrant smell of death.
And yet we played on
Not knowing where we were
Just being there
In-between your flesh mountains,
Taking another risk
And jumping together
Over an unknown abyss
With only God there for us.

Peter Corbett

Janet

She passes by with downcast eyes moving with ungainly gait,
What omniscient power ordained that such should be her fate?
To spend her days in quiescence, little sentiment to display,
Who would have thought her able of planning to seize the day?

In her tender years she would trespass in homes unwittingly
Indulgence was the gesture that gave this child such liberty.
No sibling solace to guide her, each knew that she was prone,
To live a solitary simple life where she would always be alone.

Now the fullness of her figure affirms her obvious womanhood,
Do sisterly cycles of the moon make the changes understood?
Did dreams of loves fulfilment make her restive with her life?
Or did she disbelieve, when told, she would never make a wife?

On the day she disappeared there was concern as to her plight,
Who would have thought her capable to have really taken flight?
For a brief time she was absent until perceived to be quite near,
With children and a strange young man, all else remains unclear.

She passes by very much the same as she always did before,
Perceptibly, she communicates and attempts not to withdraw.
The awareness in her manner baffles those who know her well,
Perhaps what she now knows fulfils a dream she cannot tell.

William Carr

Liverpool City Of Culture 2008

Come to Liverpool and see the great buildings
that portray our history.
King John gave Liverpool its name.
Throughout the world, Liverpool has found its fame,
For its many talents, in so many ways.
Its music, the sounds of the Beatles fill the air,
bringing happiness everywhere.
Two Cathedrals stand tall and proud,
you must admit this is so rare, to have one to spare.
Two football teams, the reds and the blues
everyone knows them, you need no clues.
Our River Mersey, with its many ships,
even the event of the 'Tall Ships',
is something no one should miss.
The Mersey Tunnel where transport travels *below*
the Mersey, children travel in awe and bliss!
The majestic St George's Hall stands gracefully
in famous Lime Street.
We have three buildings known as the Three Graces,
Then the famous Aintree, the Grand National
and all the races.

We could go on and on to tell about the City of Liverpool
and its many beautiful sights, but by coming on a visit
you will be filled with delight.

Eileen W O'Brien

Untitled

Terrible are the days without you,
Nothing is fine without you,

Thoughts other than you are very few!
Life is bitter more than a wine without you.

Missing the lovely smile of you,
Remembering every mile I walked with you.

Innocent I am, what I did to you,
Days you are not meeting are many and not a few!

I asked the winds, 'Who shook the darling buds of May?
Did you meet her on your way?'

I know you don't love me, but I really do,
At least say a lie that, 'I miss you.'

In my thoughts, is only you!

Atul Parab

Better Batter

The first time I made pancakes
You should have seen the mess
Up the wall, down the floor
All over my new dress

The second time was better
I only burnt the pan
The fire brigade came calling
Oh what a handsome man

The third time, even better
Just set the house on fire
My mother wasn't happy
The consequences dire

At last the perfect recipe
But now I need to diet
Twelve pancakes is a party
I'd better keep it quiet

Pat Ammundsen

Judgement

People judge from far and wide,
They judge the people of other sides.
Why do people judge us so,
Do they not see the person below?

To some, their judgement is based on looks,
To others, it's if you read books.
Maybe it's the way we talk,
Or maybe breathe or sing or walk.

Do they do it just for fun,
Or do they do it to see us run?
They can do it without hitting,
It's just as painful as the skitting.

Most of the time they get a warning,
So then you're dreading the next morning.
You try to avoid them through the day,
But they find you anyway.

They make you wish you'd not been born,
'Cause by the end you feel so worn.
You cannot stand the endless fight,
The nightmares wake you in the night.
Just when you think they've gone,
They turn round, come back and carry on.

You see no point in standing there,
Why do people stand and stare?

Do they find you so amusing,
Or will they look and start accusing?
We feel that we will not be heard,
We sit there in the dark and scared.

I am judged upon my looks, I am judged if I am smart,
I am judged the way I talk,
I am judged the way I walk.
Why will you not let me be?
You cannot judge if you don't know me!

Abigail Flynn (13)

My Mum, Liverpool

She looked out for me when mine couldn't be there.
From day one, she enveloped me in a blanket of care.
People who don't know her, say she's loud.
But I'm a scouser and of that I'm so bloody proud.

As a soldier I have travelled the world, far and wide.
Seen so many conflicts, but it's under her apron I return to hide.
Like any mother she cares about her son,
Especially now they've put me in charge of a gun.

I try so hard to keep up her good name,
She told me early on that life was not a game.
So I'm just one of her sons, out to make my mark.
I'd love to sail down the Mersey on Noah's Ark.

Rocks have been thrown at her so many times,
I couldn't convey them all just in one of my rhymes.
Just look at the dockers and how they were misled,
But it's on her bosom they nestle their head.

We have two great football teams, both doing her so proud.
Whether a red or a blue, we all shout for her so loud.
Legends have come and legends have gone.
All of her legends remember where they've come from.

Yes, it's true we sometimes let ourselves down,
The yob and the thief do flourish in this town.
But like any good mother, she doesn't turn her back,
She just widens her shoulders and she takes the flack.

Tom Roach

Mum

I sit and wonder why, Mum,
Just why you had to die?
Life can be so cruel, you see,
Mum, I need you here with me.
I wish I could have a chat with you.
You could tell me, Mum, just what to do.

For I am scared that I won't cope,
I know your words would give me hope.
As these months are passing by
It's getting harder. It makes me cry.
And when I think it will be years
That makes my eyes fall lots of tears.

But I know I have to be strong, Mum,
But I'm cross at God for going wrong.
I'm sad for my sister and brother
For I know how much they miss their mother.

All I have now are memories of you
But I would just like to say,
I really love and miss you.

Kerry Hart

Chemistry

You walk into the room, you catch me unaware
I feel a certain chemistry, look up and see you there.

I try to hide my feelings, I try not to react,
But my body does betray me and gives away my act.

My heart starts racing at an incredible pace,
And I feel the blush as it appears on my face.

The tension is almost tangible as it hangs there in mid-air,
The sense of exhilaration, of excitement and of fear.

Coyly I get up and slowly leave the room,
I return moments later as my composure does resume.

As I enter, you look around and then you catch my stare.
We gaze at each other awkwardly as you turn and take a chair.

I wait for my opportunity to engage you in a friendly chat,
But when I do, my words are wrong and that's the end of that.

I linger a little longer, determined not to give in,
However, the odds are stacked against me and I feel I cannot win.

Fate then intervenes and deals a final crushing blow,
As I am called away and unable to return before you go.

I see you leave the building and walk out, beyond the gate,
Yet again, opportunity passes me by, because my timing is too late.

If it's written in the stars, our paths will again someday collide,
Then there'll be no escaping me, you'll be right here at my side.

Robert Shorey

Oh, Mighty Lord

Oh! Mighty Lord
Jesus Christ

As we see You
Come for the innocence
On Pegasus' back
Riding high, bare back
The thunder and lightning strike
Right across the sky worldwide
Our Lord will appear

His hand will strike down
And for mercy
We will beg

But for the Christian
Who has gained
His love with fellowship
And given all His love

He will not be afraid
For He knows
A better place
They will go.

Debbie Storey

Untitled

The ever booze
the ever satisfying smoke
the ever music
lilting its beauty.
To come through to this gateway -
In another desert I have come through
In another sea . . .
To make the music of life
Dance before the ever death.

Life with the Spirit is
one broken victory
after another.

Paul Barron

A Breath Of Fresh Air In Formby

Child racing along
In the pinewoods, on a day out and about
A look of concentration on her face
Her pace kicks the dry sand dust
Till feet in white trainers rapidly
Taking on the colours of the dirt track.
Before she leaves this wonderland place
She is not going back without a squirrel
Captured on camera by Mum or Dad.

Prepared to be a friend to woodland creatures
Proper feed was bought at the entrance
To the nature reserve
A little fellow comes down for a treat
And nibbles a dainty bite.
Out of sight she silently stands
Excited and scarcely daring to breathe
Entranced as the camera got him in the frame
Before they go home on the train.
She has an ice cream cone
Stood with a smile
Formby is a good place to go
For all the family in the school holidays.

Freda Grieve

The Broken House

The fires are coming to eat the walls away,
The empty feeling leaves new foundations to lay.
The house again falling; I must find some solid land,
I'm tired of rebuilding upon soft wet sand.

The plans seem so solid, although there is one major flaw,
The materials to rebuild this house don't exist anymore.
I can build a false exterior with a sharp sounding bell,
Though inside just a cracked, rotting, empty shell.

The false exterior will fool all but a few,
As they look upon it they miss the walls so blue.
My garden's plush; my grass so green,
Though through blue-tinted windows this can't be seen.

I must sack my interior designers although they mean so well,
Their idea of Heaven is my idea of Hell.
The interior of your house should state who you are,
Not just to yourself but to people from afar.

If I can redecorate with all my care and grace,
People may again notice the love within my face.
I think I can rebuild this house with fire sprinklers built in,
And I'll cast away old blueprints along with all my sin.

A Wilkinson

Chapters

There are chapters in her life she would much rather forget,
Many different stories to tell, many equal regret.
No more love to give, no more tears to cry,
No more life to live, she was left to die.
Spared her life but left with the pain,
But once again it became too much a strain.
Yet she carried on, her pain she bore,
Still frozen, deep down in her core.
Now her book is closed, nothing more to tell,
The story of how she rose and then, she fell.
Although inside she is still cold,
It's time to let her wings unfold.

Sarah Jane Davies

My Hometown

Grey concrete flows into the grey buildings
to join the grey skies above.
Litter blows by on a gentle sombre breeze,
and seagulls chase scraps from kerbsides.

I walk my heavy walk watching other feet
shuffle by, dodging the bubblegum path of youth.
Listless breath makes images on the icy air
as a dewdrop rests on the end of my nose.

The industrial chimney with billowing clouds,
fill the town with the scent of poverty.
Children inhale and the frail exhale
too tired to carry on much longer.

A rusting bicycle lies on the mud
next to a shopping cart filled with lost dreams.
Graffiti on the bridge tells me
Stonz has been here.

The murky water casts reflections
of high rise flats with washing lines
full of cloths of cleansed conscience
and pristine aprons of tired mothers.

Outside my door turning the key
I take one more look behind.
Wipe away the dewdrop along with the memories.
This is my hometown, my blood
I will never be free.

Jeni Gidney

River Kent

The canoeist marvelled at how fast he went,
When paddling down the river Kent,
Though it only stretches for twenty odd miles,
It's the second fastest flowing river in the British Isles.

It cannot match the performance of the River Severn's
On its minute journey from Kentmere to just below Levens,
But it boasts a bore on the incoming tides that can be a sight,
Then again, only miniature in comparison with the Severn's might.

This smaller version is still an attraction to come and see,
As its harsh deposits cut a deeper vein down to the sea,
Over spectacular weirs, under bridges, from fast to still,
Like Barley Bridge at Staveley, then quietly past the old woodmill.

Over the weir here and it meanders westerly - then turns south - going wild,
As it's joined by the River Gowan just outside the 'Eagle and Child',
Then speedily down to Bowston, Burneside - joined then by the River Mint.

Under seven bridges as it passes through Kirkbie Kendale,
called Kendal today,
Past Abbot Hall, Lound and Natland roads as it wends on its way,
Past Sedgwick and the water level measuring device - 'Force Fall',
Measuring the flow before going past the sedate old Levens Hall.

Not far to go now, down twixt Arnside and Grange over Sands
and the Bay,
One of the most beautiful twenty odd miles that anyone can portray,
You might well say that it flows too fast to capture the beauty in full,
But to us it's still a magnet with one heck of a pull.

Jack Edwards

With Me

Before me, lies the beauty of an ocean;
and laid before me, is the wonder of the sea.
Far above me, towers the majesty of mountains;
in my sight, they stand so elegant and free.

In the dawning, I see a blue sky hanging over me,
with the darkness - my velvet mantle for the night.
Stars twinkle soft, high above me in the heavens;
as they cast their beacon, of tiny glowing light.

I see the distant rolling hills - of my fair homeland;
with lush meadows, the striking colour of emerald green.
There's lakes: there's streams: there's flowing rivers,
with each one wearing, a coat of silver sheen.

I see vast forests, adorned with all beautiful greenery;
On a carpet of bluebells, in the early light of spring.
Our feathered friends I see - as God's tiny miracles;
as on high perches, their sweet song warmly rings.

I've noticed wondrous miracles, all around me,
they unfold each time the night turns into day,
And I marvel, at the colours in a rainbow;
when the sun and rain decide to share their play.

In the summer time, my admiration lays in nature's garden
for there's so much striking beauty, all around.
These qualities, are like treasure laid before me;
when Heaven joins earth, upon this common ground.

My sight has held so many incredible wonders;
but I'd give up everything, and all that I can see.
And my eyes would crave for nothing, but the darkness;
if you could no longer walk upon this earth, with me.

Thomas Ian Graham

A Leaf In A Storm

Life is a roller coaster
With its painful highs and lows.
We are carried along like
A leaf in a storm,
Unable to stop the flow.
Then, as the storm and the wind abates
And a calmness descends on the earth,
We open our eyes and see that joy
Has been there . . .
      Waiting -
         Hoping
            Giving birth.

Life goes on, no matter what befalls this world,
With traumas every day.
But somehow, storms and sadness add
A strength to how we pray.
We learn to hold on steadfastly
Watch little acorns grow;
So . . .
Nurture, love and cherish life
      Catch the leaf -
         Hold on tight -
            Don't let go.

Judy Rochester

Beautiful In Your Sadness

I've never seen anyone
So beautiful in their sadness
As you with hair that softly shines
In ringlets fair, framing a face
Made delicate, lost in sorrow;
With a soft mouth speaking mutely
Of grief and blue-eyes that sparkle,
Flickering in the light, with tears.
I speak; 'No!' - I have never seen
Anyone so beautiful,
Beautiful in their sadness,
As you.

Katie Boyd

Confused? You Will Be

Is it love,
Or not?
How can I love him
When I don't even know him?
Why is this
So confusing?
Help!

Jenny Messenger

Two Sights

We open our eyes for visions of planet earth
A child crying, joining us the first day of birth
Persons passing, smiles on their faces, talking
To maybe a loved one, arm in arm, walking
Colours of all kinds blending our sight
From early morning to late dust at night
Patterns of things as they pass our way
As the hours tick along the hourly day
Yet we see what should never be seen
Where evil is black and never grass green
Wars of red blood, people never seeing again
Who lived a life but not time of age to gain
Man, woman and child, who wanted only life
Part of a majority who meet strife
Ones only rich in feelings and thought
Who work, parents, teachers taught
To love their neighbour as themselves
Yet exists the evil ones that delves
Into sins that should never be seen
Their minds corrupt, many years been
To close your eyes to such, can be done
But would this war of sins, be ever won?
That make those we see laughing, die
Bringing sorrow and tears to the eye
Can our sights make peace, be bought
By making those that are evil be taught
That they see by sight, good around
Splendour of nature and humans found
Blue skies, green fields, people living
To their planet, earth returns, giving
To be born, living their life's span
Unspoilt by any other living human.

Brian Frost

For Mam

Loving and caring,
Always sharing,
You'll always be
In my heart,
Nothing can ever
Change a thing,
We will never be apart.
I'll love you forever,
I know you love me,
Let's stay together
For all eternity.

Stephanie Williamson (8)

Requiem Of A Child

The Crematorium is so bitter, cold and unwelcoming,
It's just like school. 'Be quiet and sit there very still.'
Music from a mighty organ somewhere, is softly playing,
As we shuffle and squeak in rows, we all quickly fill.
In wonder, the silent space feels as if it is the sky
That's full of nothing, patiently waiting for the sun.
For we are here because my little gran has died.
I don't know where she's gone, in tears my mum
Yet silently. It frightens me, it's so unlike her not to smile.
As we wait, a strange man talks, others weep
And sniffle in the coldness.
I have Gran in my head, she would think this was vile,
'You're too young to understand,' they said. 'She was very old.'
We watch the coffin, as through the curtains it slowly goes
To music she didn't like.
I feel her smile, hear her funny laugh. Her lovely warm knee.
Mum says, 'She's gone now,' But I don't think she knows
How I saw her pain last week as she kissed and cuddled me.
I'm not sad, but lonely. Together we had such special days.
'Be brave for us,' she's saying to me softly, 'you're so very much
                                                                                   like me.'

George Carrick

La Vida Es Una Perra

Through all of life's uncertainties
On fragile wings we fly
We cling to hope and sweet desire
Until the day we die

To those who cause anxiety
To those who we adore
To all who shape our restless lives
We wish we'd said much more

Dreams that linger unfulfilled
Will haunt us to the end
Tempered by the memories of
Each true and honest friend

This life's a journey, filled with pain
A selfish, twisted game
Good hearts will wish forever
That we were all the same

Be thankful for the moments
That stand out from the rest
Remember as the cloud descends
You were among the best

John Robinson

Belonging

Lonely
I sit atop the fell
emptiness
clothes my being
space
absorbs my mind
my soul is free
the universe
my garden where
thoughts can grow, where
perception can envelop
this sphere of Earth
and nurture it . . .
peace has no equal
here there is no loneliness
I have returned home . . .

Carolyn Smith

Global Warming

I look up at the sky, mean, cold and dark
There are floods in the park
Nobody stirs, they're all in their houses
Tucked away with their cosy spouses
They have children playing
Can't you hear what I am saying?

The creatures are out here, bracing the floods
They have to cope in the hills and woods
Children can't play anymore
Because they rarely go out the door
Do they know of these other lives?
With just as much right to husbands and wives

If it's not a dry summer, it's horrendous gales
Maybe the food supply fails
Each year you see less of this or that
It may be a butterfly, swallow or bat
So what's the solution to this global mess
Be resigned to the outcome of evolution, I guess?

John Foster

Lakeland Fells

Cumbrian Fells have names like these:
Maiden Moor and Gavel Nese,
Aaron's Slack and Moses' Trod;
Crinkle Crags and Starling Dodd.
Winter Crag, Bracken Rigg, Blaeberry Hill,
Hell Gate Screes and Rossett Ghyll.

Nitting Haws, Brown Knotts and Lady's Rake
All stand high above Derwent Lake.
Measand, Mellbreak, Great Mickledore
And Mallerstang edge where the buzzards soar.
There's Hanging Stone and Catstycam,
Camspout Crags and Wetherlam.

Were Romans alert on Roman Fell?
What story could Nine Standards tell?
Leading to Hardknott from Wrynose Pass
Goes the Roman road to Ravenglass.
Then tramp Swirl How, Seatallan, over Black Sail
To the sounding sea beyond Ennerdale.

John R Parker

Cumbria

Come to Rheged in the hill
All around the mountains spill
Lakes below, tranquil and still
Grasmere, Derwent, Ullswater too
Climb a fell, drink in the view.
Walk and walk, a hundred stiles
Feel peace and calm for miles and miles.
One hour, wild fast moving cloud
Then sun burns off the misty shroud
To reveal a land, drenched in sun
The only sound; a wild bee's hum.
Stone farms peep aside a ghyll
A trickling stream babbles its fill
Bleating sheep and bracken rustle
Far away the small town bustle.
I live here and feel at rest
Cumbria a county blessed!

Jennifer H Fox

Immaculate Potential

Thus I follow'd the star
Shining though it did
Brightly with delusion.
Thus came I upon the scene
The emanation of God
Fast became mine confusion.
Innocence hath such promise
Just as death
Be the consequence of life.
Thus I quit the scene
Uncertainty mine companion
Long mine journey.
Such immaculate potential
Such divine intention
Such bewildering conclusion.

Sam Dixon

It's Up To You/Sing For Justice

I watched you sing for justice
To put an end to pain and sorrow,
I watched you play for freedom
With a passion like there's no tomorrow.

Joining hands and hearts across the world
We are one from Britain to the USA,
Uniting to make poverty, history
So that thousands can live one more day.

No matter how many miles are between us
I'll cross bridges, climb mountains, swim seas,
To join hands with you, hear your voice
To help innocent children become free.

A million voices, heard tonight as one
To achieve hope for which so many strive,
I'm supporting a cause I believe in
And the bonus was seeing you live.

We'll continue to fight for their freedom
From the UK, America and other nations too,
So come on G8 leaders, we've done our bit
The rest is now up to you.

Margaret Ann Scott

A Tempestuous Night

As I lay my head down to sleep
Thunderous thoughts into my head do creep
The worries and workings of the day
In my mind havoc they do play
I toss and turn trying to rest
But all I hear is the pounding in my chest
Oh how I wish sleep would come
Now that the day is really done
On into the early hours I lie
Looking at the dark night sky
Soon the daylight will appear
This is when sleep will come, I fear
The clock on the shelf says it's time to rise
It's going to be hard to open my sleepy eyes
I hope today will be a better one
As I don't wish to have it to dwell upon
When to bed I have to go
I must fix my mind on a peaceful flow.

J Parker

To Mother With Love

My mother is a person I admire and love
But sadly now, she looks down from above
I loved the way she never shouted
Yet her wishes, no one ever flouted.

She ruled us with a fist in a tender glove,
And every day we felt her love.

Guests were welcomed and they filled the house
Although there were many, she never groused.
She'd greet everyone with a cheery smile
And however busy, she would chat for a while.

When I married, I had to leave home,
My husband's job was 200 miles away.
Although I was happy, I missed my mother.
I thought of her many times a day.

Though no longer with me, except in spirit,
My love and respect for her, knows no limit.

Jean Wood

My Countdown Dilemma

At last I'm here on Countdown
It really is a thrill
To make long words from letters
And to test my number skill

For weeks and weeks I've pondered
How best to play the game
Which tactics I have wondered
Guarantee a champion's fame

One large one and five small ones
Or two big ones and four small
Shall I let Carol make the choice
I'm just not sure at all

The numbers could be easy
Yet again they may be hard
I daren't lack concentration
Or I might miss 'leotard'

Will my mind go blank and fail me
Or will I do just fine
Suppose I only manage three
When I want to get a nine

The conundrum may elude me
I might make a mistake
Will I use a word that's not allowed?
Calm down for goodness sake

But whatsoe'er may happen
I'll have a super time
And should I not appear again
At least you've heard my rhyme

Christine Skeer

Changing Views

The yellow-tipped fingers reach up skyward
Each one trying to outshoot the other
Red ones like painted nails bend and drape
Gracing the ground as they wither

The time of the snowdrop is ending
As they make way for birds and their brood
Robins are dancing through plant life
As the earth and nature lift the mood

Magnolia trees are showing their powder puff pinks
On the otherwise bare tree
As life spews from every corner
Crevice and cave, the eyes of the hawk see me

He perches high above, a king upon a throne
This silent world of his, he rules, all alone
And then by chance, a passing glance,
His sight will rest upon his prey
Majestic he leads a merry dance
As he lures it far away from safety and family
It's food for him today

Hawthorn hedge is bustling,
Birds busy in song and chatter
Ignoring the walker and the dog
Pretending that I don't matter
They need to spread the word
Tell all that spring is here
Declare a change of season
Their song, symphonic to my ear

Sandra Roberts

Snowdrops At Rode Hall

Cold winds blow across the landscape,
Tiny white heads bob in unison.
Follow the paths, see nature's gifts.
Tread where many have trodden before.
Trees provide some shelter from frost.
Go and explore each nook and cranny
And marvel at the sights you see,
Just count the number of White Ladies.
How many bulbs have been planted?
You are transported to paradise
As you wander down Snowdrop Walk.
Rode Hall looks down on the visitors,
Welcoming them to its secrets
Hidden among those winding pathways.
'Do come back next year,' it calls,
As you start making your way back home.
Snowdrops herald the start of spring,
Your spring started right here at Rode Hall.

Angela Pritchard

Childhood Refugee

The bread and butter of two decades
Hailed as 'the best of your life'
Diminished into bite-size chunks.
Endless summers and sheltered winters
Turn grey and curl into themselves.
Their fallibility and frailty
Shock transitional figures with
Their innovative, gradual fall.
Prompting refugees from childhood to
Seek institutional asylum with erratic ecstasy.

Applications, decisions and doors
Occupy time like shrinking toddlers.
Responsibility thrust upon wide eyes
And open mouths that used to do the shrieking.

Weeks with go-faster stripes
Relentlessly pulse.
The heart of existence is
Soon to be dislodged.
Native tongues will become distorted,
Everyday furniture will become
Sporadic revivals of time passed,
Rejuvenated, then neatly packed away
Again in-between increasingly
Creased tissue paper.

Jennifer Hill

For The Love Of My Dad

Dad had immense strength for me,
He fought so hard to stay.
The time came when he went away,
I asked so many times, why this way?

A man who cared for others,
Gave all he had to make others happy.
He was shunned by a sister and two brothers,
When he was sad, I tried to make him happy.

I wanted to do so many things in life,
More for my dad to make him glad.
He lived his life so I wouldn't be sad,
Now I must go on and live for my dad.

It won't be the same without him,
My dad made me what I am.
My thanks to him would be
To raise my family in honour of him.

Wendy Wilkinson

My Friend Teresa

I had a friend for over thirty years
And I remember times we both shed tears
But together we trod a beautiful line
She truly was a friend of mine

When I was down she was always there
All my troubles she'd gladly share
I was glad to be her private clown
To wipe away that seldom frown

Loyalty came without a price
And her words came straight from the heart
To have such friendship and devotion
I just prayed we'd never part

But time has closed our book of life
And we've come to our rainbow's end
In everyone's life the stack of cards falls
And I have lost my very best friend

Now no one will ever fill her space
And sadness is the price you pay
For to know I'll never hold her in my arms again
Cuts me more than mere words can say

So enjoy the carousel of life
Catch happiness when it's thrown
Stand together through troubled times
Because in the end we all have to sleep alone

Graham Bowers

The Cyclamen

It sits upon my window sill
Better than any anti-depressant pill
As I sip my morning cup of tea
I am fascinated by what I see.

Rising above the mirror pot
Sits a bulb or corm, I know not what
From the crowded centre shoots push forth
Growing and jostling for all their worth.

At first I cannot really tell
If leaf or flower is emerging well
But very soon it is clear to me
The difference now easy to see.

The leaf at first is closed, dark and small
As it opens and grows it turns lighter and tall
The upper leaf pattern inspires the best art nouveau
Or the finest lace formed in a circular row.

What thrills me even more
Is the way the twisted petals rise and form a core
With arched head that backwards bursts
Like Japanese fans, bright pink at first.

As leaves and flowers fade and die
New shoots form and vie
For their deserved place in the sun
The cycle of life continues its run.

Theresa M Carrier

Saint Nicholas

Dear Santa, I would like to write
And tell you of my awful plight
Had to move this year and so
I now live in a bungalow

So getting down the chimney's out
The rumours are you're rather stout
I'll leave the patio door unlocked
Your sleigh no doubt will be quite stocked

The pies are by the big stone cup
And of course a glass of wine to sup
So if you are going to hang about
Be good and put the milk bottles out

I hope that Rudolph's full of cheer
Last year he had a cold, poor deer
Little wonder his nose is red
Should have been tucked up in bed

Oh hope you got my wanted list
Can't think of anything I've missed
I really have been good and sweet
When you call I'll be fast asleep

Esmond Simcock

By The Sea

Soft sand on the tide,
Orange drifts instead of blue,
And it's good that it's silent except for the sea,
No one moaning or upsetting me.
All is calm now, so serene,
Forget the past, what might have been.
All the time my heart was here.
Wind in my hair,
Touching my face,
And the sun's warm mantle around me
Like an old friend.

C Rowley

A Stranger In The Street

Yesterday I noticed someone standing solo in the street,
Studying the ground, kicking litter by his feet.
His leather face told a history I knew he couldn't repeat,
A tale of pain and hurt, which my ears will never meet.

Yesterday I saw a man standing vacant by the road,
Watching the floor as if he had already told
Of the pain upon his face so empty, so cold,
Standing still, soft and silent, so brave, so bold.

Today I went to visit him, the stranger in the street,
A person I've been watching, the man I've wanted to meet.
His somber face seemed open, to anything or anyone,
He met my eye and smiled at me as I introduced myself at once.

Katie Cheetham

Bonnie Scotland

If you've never been to Scotland,
You don't know what you've missed,
The grandeur of the mountains
Even seen through rain or mist.

The beauty of the lochs
With the sun shining on the water,
If you have never been to Scotland,
Then I think it's time you oughta.

The miles of deep green forests,
And the glens with their running burns,
The beautiful Highland cattle,
There is loveliness wherever you turn.

The moors when full of heather
And the wonderful golden broom,
Stretching for miles along the highway,
A sight to dispel the gloom.

Scotland is steeped in history,
Such as the Battle of Bannockburn,
The massacre of Glencoe,
And the birth of Robbie Burns.

Then there was Mary, Queen of Scots,
Beheaded by Elizabeth's hate,
And Bonnie Prince Charlie fleeing to Skye
To escape the same dreadful fate.

The Scots are very proud people
And they are kind and helpful too,
They make you feel very welcome,
So how about a visit or two?

Phyllis Ing

Fear

I live in fear
As each day dawns
Not knowing what the day will bring
Doors left open wide
For anyone who cares to enter
Sometimes floorboards creak
As if someone upstairs
Walks the floor
I'm told I'm paranoid
But no one knows
What I feel inside

Alice Higham

The Four Of Us

(Ronald Frank Astell died on May 28th 2005. Of those of us you left behind, we shall never forget, we send our fondest love and best wishes to you and Mum)

A Worthwhile Struggle

Night school to catch up with figures of the past,
Accountancy and bookkeeping kept me busy,
So was a young family starting up.
Working hard behind the bar,
From courting couple to a worthwhile struggle.
Two sons of whom I am so proud,
We both agreed, Iris and I (for once!)
The four of us in a safe, secure home,
We watched as more families grew,
Nigel with sons David, Simon and James,
Trevor with Mary had Thomas and Rosin.
As I kept in touch with my dear sister Pansy and husband Bill,
I always forgot whose turn it was to phone!
Barbara's family so close too,
Friends and neighbours kept me strong,
Housekeeper and friend Chris helped me so,
A good companion in Kathy, I thank you.
As in later years of physical damage,
I always seemed to stay so alert and active,
Legs slowed down just a little you know,
Walking sticks and hearing aid a must.
A walk to see an old friend laid to rest no more,
Because at last I can travel on my last trip,
To visit my beloved high up, waiting in the heavens above.
I have missed you Iris, oh so much,
Together my darling,
Dust to dust.

Nigel Astell

Padstow Born But No Bread

An angry look is etched on Nicola's face
god damn tourists have emptied the place,
Round and round the aisles she goes
to other customers angry glances she throws,
Not a tin nor a loaf of bread in her sight
the manager she wants to throttle and smite,
In the meat section she should have known
this too had been stripped to the bone,
Through a crowd were spied Coke and pop
but when she arrived there wasn't a drop,
So when in Padstow you tourists beware
some people do actually have to live there!

Ian Jobson

Liverpool, My Liverpool

A ride through the city, and what did I find?
The future before me, the past was behind.
How sad was the feeling with what I did view,
The old Liverpool I loved was replaced with the new.
The great concrete buildings all standing aloof,
Like a jungle of wrath without any proof.
The shops that I loved, Jeromes, Jacksons, Nanettes,
Dubarrys, and oh all the rest were to let.
All stark and bare, boarded up, 'For Sale'.
The price of inflation had taken its toll.
I looked all around me like a stranger abroad,
Then looked before me to the long, open road,
And as far as I wandered down memory lane,
I know in my heart I'll not see again
The Liverpool I knew when I was a girl,
A city of laughter, a bright shining pearl.
The Grafton and Reeces, our isle of Capri,
Where we danced to the music of My Belle Ami
On the New Brighton ferry, with hearts full of love,
Tho' we hadn't a penny, the sun shone above.
And now as I see it, a stranger I feel,
Where I grew up, it seems so unreal.
The wealth of a city I once knew and loved
Had vanished completely as though it had moved.
But deep as I thought of all that had passed
And of all the enchantment that somehow got lost,
And of this generation perhaps one day they'll find,
The future's before you, the past is behind.

Joan Harris

Transparent Peace

Transparent line, delicately suspended
Only visible by illuminated crystal dew tears
To fall from the visible - deep oblivion
The journey over-intensifies the implications of truth
Wanting to reach an unmeasured, invisible cavity which would
alter hopelessness
Opening a doorway into a complicated existence - an
isolated emptiness
An abandoned stillness - a transformation receding into the
deepness of eternal solace
A substitute to the suffocating transience of time, intricate
yet endless
Dew tears evaporate or descend into the void
Sanctuary behind the eyes that no one sees, until tears show the
hidden emotion
Reminders are soon forgotten, yet a ghost of a witness remains
until it too is forgotten
The sanctuary offers a consolation, yet to pass through the doorway
to be enclosed into the innermost sanctuary, are we not avoiding life
to attain peace?
Reaching out along the crystal line exposing oneself
Wanting to embrace that faint energy which is fast disappearing -
peace

Hilary Jean Clark

Unamused

The creative tremors rumble the crust of my mind
as the lava of inspired sentient thought unrefined
flows from the subconscious sea in fever-fits of rhymes.
Cryptic flashes of random inspiration always seem to coincide
with the knocking of the muse who finds that access is denied.
The psycho-active barricade that the chemicals provide
is a narcotic unreality where the poet may hide.

William Anthony Ralphson

The Vision

Sitting alone on a desolate shore,
dreaming of days long gone by.
Feeling I wasn't alone anymore
a 'vision' was catching my eye.
She stood there before me,
her attributes clear, she must
have emerged from the sea.
Then I beheld her beautiful eyes,
the colour of which puzzled me,
the green was a hue not found in the skies,
maybe dredged from the depth of the sea.
I'd never before encountered this shade,
a new opalescence of green,
an exclusive off-shoot of purest jade,
the like of which I'd never seen.
Strong the attraction, resisting was tough,
although I approached her with caution,
she receded from me, quickly enough, and
'melted' back into the ocean.

Bill Austin

Angels

I believe in angels, I believe they are there
Waiting and watching, the unseen stare,
As they hope that we will each see them
Find under the flower petal the stem,
Strong and true, they shine their light
Out into the deepest blackness of night.
Like a beacon beckoning to humankind
Who with eyes to see, nevertheless are blind.

But as we live on into the new millennium
Be aware, their angelic time will come.
They will be seen, their song will be heard.
They're waiting to be summoned by inviting words
By the ones that have the knowledge, they await
The future that is coming, when destiny meets fate.
We humans at last reach out with spiritual thought
To join with our angels in communion consciously sought.

Carolina de la Cruz

Ash Tree In My Hedge

Tree of all trees, the ash tree in my hedge
A calendar to mark the changing year
With winter branches etched against the sky
While skeins of geese migrating southward fly
In tightly knit formation in a wedge.

Come the spring, the ash tree in my hedge
Shows coal-black buds and hopeful we recite
'Oak before ash, only a splash
Ash before oak, then a soak.'
Then suddenly from one day to the next
The green shoots come, fulfilment of a pledge.

In summer time the ash tree spreads its leaves
Thick and green to shelter bird and beast
And mutes the sounds of traffic on the road
A tree to view with reverence and awe
For there is magic in the spell it weaves.

In autumn other leaves spread brown and gold
The ash tree waits till all this scattered wealth
Is spent, then like a tired child
Discarding clothes and shoes at one fell swoop,
Drops all. Its limbs stretch stark and cold.

And when I see my ash tree stripped of leaves
I know that soon, too soon, the days will shrink
The nights grow longer and the year's round
Will shift again till we're at winter's brink.

Mary Hodges

My Family Tied Down

O'er the hills of Lancashire
Toward the north of me
Lay a lovely tower;
Standing peacefully.
Lay an ocean of years
Many a famous face
Children skipping blissfully
So joyous and full o' grace!
'Twas there my ma did take me
When to a grasshopper I was knee-high
Many a family holiday
Cheerfully passed us by.
Summer by the sea
Me, my ma and gran
Grandad building sandcastles
Ma, seeking her perfect man!
My pa, apparently
Ran away somewhere to there
'Took his floozy with him,' Ma said
Though I never did really care.
Cos o'er the hills of Lancashire
Toward the north of me
Stands sunny Blackpool!
'Tis England's truest beauty!

Claire Smith

Death Of The King

I was there when the last loom stopped
The gate's clang was the mill's funeral bell
As flat caps and black clogs slowly moved down the street
To their homes, waiting families to tell.

The smoke-blackened walls and cobbles below
Were like sides of some dark, dismal tomb
Though no tears would be shed in those poor terraced homes
Everyone mourned the end of the loom.

Death's sarcophagi, industry's hearse
We all watched as they loaded the trucks
And we heard Cotton's death rattle as they went by
On the day instant poverty struck.

We were left with a life with no prospect, no hope
The old town was a desolate place
But the staunch northern courage of true, honest men
Put the fighting look back on our face.

So we talked and we dreamed and we fought for our lives
Now the muck and depression are gone
And we look back with pride on the place of our birth
At this Lancashire town that lives on.

Now we see tree-lined avenues, faces that smile,
We watch children play in clean air.
Though the mighty machines that sustained us are dead
I remember their death. I was there.

No regrets for the past, for the dirt and the grime
Life is good, no more sorrow or care
And the time of King Cotton is part of the past
But I still can recall, I was there!

Brian Croft

Salt Of The Earth

We are the salty grains of forebears
Measured into grammes
Of so many cups.
Some are tasted with regret,
Ill repute taints them
Like a bad smell
Down wind from the living
Not yet entombed
The only stench is hell.
Configured so
The pattern appears
Taken as said, and read
I dare you to think
Of the cold stone slabs
Glinting in the moonlight
Tread the corpses laid knee deep
Don't trip
To be sucked down
Into a deeper place
Your face never to appear again
And only the sound
Of a distant bell

Glenda Stryker

Happy Motoring In The North West

Over the hills
and not too far

our car
climbs the bleak flanks
of Ingleborough,
or takes us to
the stone arches
of Devil's Bridge,

corkscrews
through Bowland's Trough,
or round the blind bends
into Coniston,

ending where the good pubs are,
over the hills
and not too far.

Tim Hoare

Pathway Of Life

May I walk with you on your pathway of life,
I'm standing beside you just waiting to know?
I can't walk it for you, you've chosen that task,
But I'll walk it with you, all you need is to ask.

It won't be all rainbows, that's not how it goes
For there's good times and bad on everyone's road,
When storm clouds bring trouble, as bring it they must,
We can face it together if in me you'll trust.

When you suffer injustice that brings your heart low
Keep faith in my love, and be still and know,
That I see all roads, not just here and now
And my justice is perfect, I give you my vow.

So walk through the pain with your head held high,
There'll be sunshine again to light up your sky
And if it gets lonely and friends they seem few,
Remember I love you and will always be true.

Whatever your path, wherever you go
I'll be beside you much more than you know,
So walk it with patience, no envy, no strife
And walk in my peace on your pathway of life.

Susan Carr

Awaiting Death
(For Fiona)

My eyes are shut; my mouth is dry,
Sooner or later I know that I'll die.
Until that time, however, comes,
I'll lie quiet, still; I'll drop my guns.

So still I do find this peaceful breeze,
Quilting my body from head to knees.
And yet I know that I must go,
The piper's calling, I know - must go.

And yet before I leave this plain,
To avoid the suffering and the pain,
I'll try to do my best to see
The beauty of its mysteries.

Now that the summer sun has gone,
Winter's breeze shall come, anon.
This will beckon to me more
Than any piper at my door.

And when this happens, my eyes shall clear,
I'll see the meanings of the years,
And then I'll rest. I'll let go,
I'll let the wind take me for I know
That all that is bad is in turn good,
And I'll find peace like each mortal man should.

Christopher Kennedy

The Netherwoods

The river spews white horses
Steely leaves rustle and rust
Deep red veins
No longer bleed.

Alongside a graveyard
Weeping trees; bereft
In death
The Netherwoods

Grieve

Joyce Graham

The Tall Men

He stands by the canal,
Arms outstretched
And as we pass,
There is a low hum.

From a distance,
You see his frame,
Stark in the landscape.

Now you are aware,
You see them, everywhere.

Raymond Pilling

A Rare Gift

After labouring intense
Never before experienced
Everything else ceased to exist.
Except me and my world of content.
Clothed from Heaven lies
A foretaste of paradise upon my chest.
My ardent heart halts.

That moment indelible
All my yearning will not bring back.
How can I
Make them understand
What they mean to me?
Must they spring, richly pretty
In prevailing petals and hues.

Showing off like a butterfly pregnant with colour.
Perhaps I was as eager to take flight.
Widen your glorious spirit yonder.
I can give love, not my thoughts,
You have your own, make me proud.
Take care, birds will be ever hungry to snatch.
Don't forget, the door always lies open.
I will be waiting, till fit of my stone wings.

Yasmeen Ahmed

Inspiration

I'm looking for inspiration
For inspiration's a wonderful thing!
It's full of light and wonder
The world is full of it.
Colours of the rainbow!
We just have to look for it.
Children in the playground!
A flower trembling as it grows
A library full of wonder!
Beautiful landscape skies.
Fill us with a new beginning
When the day has said goodbye!
Meeting the flutter of the last bird
God's gifts of inspiration
To you and I!

E Riverside

Cracked Rainbows

Each and every one of us living
Are slowly destroying our environment
Houses built for homes create fossil fuel
Farming creates industry and in turn, jobs
Both bring carbon or sulphur dioxide
It's carried on the wind and rain
Slowly floating down on snow - formulated into
Acid rain, which brings its own destruction
Through deforestation - comes scrub land
In scrub the loss of flora and fauna
Loss of wildlife and habitation and food
Aquatic life are starved of oxygen
Geology is being eroded away
Climate change and sea levels are the warning
From what has been created - by man - for man
In turn is being wiped out drop by drop
Our fragile infrastructure is another generation's future
For us to keep tomorrow's rainbows
We must replace what we've taken for free
Power over politics - our future depends on it.

David Charles

July

July days are distant dreams
Of crowded trains in shrouds of steam
Dashing along with a clacketty beat
Away from the mills and steep cobbled streets
And into the bays of sun-kissed sands
Where there's time to waste and time to stand.
Time to sleep in candy-striped chairs
While seagulls glide and dance on air,
Caught on the breeze that playfully tweaks
Each pennant and flag on the sandcastle keep,
Bravely defying the tide's ebb and flow
Until the moment when there's nowhere to go
Trapped by the sea, locked in strands of time
Like the carousels that spin in my mind
Like the Ferris wheel that climbs through the clouds
Fragments of colour, a pastiche of sound.
Punch and Judy, the circus clown
Laughter and magic, freedom's crown.
And when somber shadows point the way home
In quiet contemplation of a happy sojourn
See how fast the rainbow fades
From gold to green, from green to grey.

Hayes Turner

Changing Tides

The playful breeze
As seasons change,
The sudden bout
Of chilly rain
A warning yet again
But warm snug fires
As nights draw in
Gardens too take their rest
Having given us
Their very best
In colour and perfume
Flowers and plants
The joyous crest
Snow and frost
Will take their place
Everything shimmering
Like silvery ghosts
Each season brings
Its own reward
A magic all its own
Woven with care
For each and everyone to share.

Margaret Parnell

The Written Word

Write down something every day,
Let not your thoughts go away,
Find yourself some paper and a pen,
Write a story, a story beginning 'Remember when'
It may be of love, it may be of strife,
Of a husband, a partner, a lover or wife.

What an art this, writing to remember,
A month, a year, a day in September,
When times were good and had to be had,
Days that were worse that left you feeling bad.
Looking towards tomorrow with no solution,
Trials, tribulations and fear of retribution.

Yet what of the times, the times that matter?
You found answers in coping, yourself you could flatter.
You looked toward compassion, 'make do and mend'
Perhaps all you needed was one true friend
To 'talk out' the problems and point the way,
Rub ointment on wounds, say, 'Have a good day.'

Ellen Spiring

Lament

I couldn't always be there,
and you wouldn't come here.
I always wanted you close,
you always wanted me near,
and the feelings I put deep inside of you,
and the switch that I flicked that rekindled past youth,
and I was the boy that I'd never been,
and I was the man with new purpose, new meaning,
and after being so high this is the fall that I feared,
and when we talk on the phone I can hear your tears,
and the soul that's been taken out of my heart,
and the heart has been ripped away from my soul,
and the dream that I dreamt of a brand new start
has been shattered again as a final recall,
and the tablets I bought and safely keep
are all the pills that I need to take -
and the feeling of unknowing, of what to do now,
is the feeling of knowing I would never wake,
and it's not through depression,
and it's not lack of self worth.
It's knowing how happy one person can be,
and knowing that happy I can't always be,
and having tasted nirvana, Utopia, Heaven,
and knowing such happiness can't go on forever,
and feeling I'm starting to bring you down
is something I cannot entertain, ever,
and, these soulmates need to return to good friends,
and our 'ships in the night' - that really must end,
and a love story written without false pretence
is a love story shared but destined to end.

Paul Anthony Scott

Spring

From fragrant spring flowers, I tasted wild honey
Swallows surfed the warm breeze.
Roses blossomed and babies' cheeks
Flushed with regeneration.
Abundant love, manifest through untempered desire;
Summon the wintered soul, from isolation to communion;
Sweeten herbs, green the vales;
Raise eternally from disintegrating rock,
Vibrant echoes
Of unaged energy.

Simon Kilshaw

My Church

My church is the great outdoors,
Its roof the dome of ever-changing sky.
Its pillars the stately trees in woodland ways,
That make the arches overhead so high.
Its choristers are birds who sing God's praise,
Treble of larks to bass voice of the rooks.
They sing from early morn to set of sun,
Sermons there are, in stones,
Books in the running brooks.
Its floor the meadow grass so lush and green,
With wild flowers blossoming so sweet and fair,
And everywhere the face of God is seen,
Its organ is the wind that plays the air.
My church is vast and stretches far and wide,
With seasons as its gospels, four to learn.
From moorland's loneliness, to seashore's tide,
I see God's work wherever I may turn.
In woodland's shades or mountain's rocky face,
This is my church, no building takes its place.

Margaret B Baguley

Someone To Care

Lonely and old, that's what you see,
    all that you feel is pity for me.
You live, you laugh, you love then you smile
    at my foibles and whims and you humour awhile.
But you haven't noticed, you just haven't seen
    the type of person I am and have been.
I'm not just old, threadbare and worn,
    with tatty old slippers and cardi' that's torn.
I'm real, I'm human, I'm flesh and I'm feeling.
    I've a long life behind me and a story worth hearing.
I've had family and friends, I've had lovers and foes.
    I've shared in their joys and many a woe.
I've fought and I've cared, I've loved and I've lost
    but better than that I've lived at all cost.
Yet you still haven't noticed, you just cannot see
    the person that built the old woman that's me.
A daughter; a lover; a wife and a mother;
    many people, one body, that holds them together.
Those people are still here, a big part of me.
    Please don't ignore them, listen and see.
I'm real, I'm human, I'm flesh and I'm feeling.
    This isn't a baby with which you are dealing.
The life that's behind me still lingers in mind.
    The life that's before me marks more than just time.
So pay some attention and think carefully,
    the person you're nursing isn't just me.
It's you in the future when this is your past,
    when your life's gone behind you and you're breathing your last.
What will you wish for when you're sitting here?
    For a painless death or a life that's carefree?
Trust me, trust me, the difference is there
    and that difference is made having someone who cares.

Linda Howitt

Metamorphosis

See the patch of eggs
Underneath the leaf
The caterpillar
Tell-tale sign reveals.

Grub becomes entombed
In gossamer skin
Protective cocoon
Can't see what's within.

Soon the change begins
Shaping, transforming,
To turn and gain wings.
New body warming.

I spy butterfly,
Beautiful and bright,
As all breathe a sigh,
So graceful in flight.

Lesley J Worrall

Out Of Sight

Why is it there?
For what
its whirling destiny?

Crazy angle planet
racing around
just out of sight

at the impossible
periphery of the known
solar system.
Entity
complete unto itself?
Or exultant with the knowing -
the ecstasy - of running rings
in secrecy around us all?

For what
its whirling destiny?
How, where and *why*
is it there just out of sight?

Chris Creedon

Ode To Black Pudding Chucking

Black pudding chucking dates back to the days of the Wars
                                                    of the Roses
When the Lancastrians ran out of cannon balls they would
Stuff their cannon full of black puddings and fire them at the enemy
The Yorkshire pudding at which the black puddings are chucked
Is really a Yorkist musketeer in disguise?
But after having black puddings chucked at him for over a
                                    hundred and thirty years
He has either been battered to death or died of old age

Black pudding chucking, black pudding chucking
You set the farmers' wives a-clucking
The very sight of such waste meat
Is worse than a million smelly feet

Philip Corbishley

Untitled

I have sat and cried for the way I have felt
I have questioned God for the cards I've been dealt
I have wept for the person I was last year
I have prayed for the mist in my eyes to be cleared
I have wanted to die and not given a damn
I have done things I shouldn't and tried every scam

The thirst for heroin is no longer within
I've made my choice and I won't let it win
It's always there in the back of my brain
Desperately trying to drive me insane
Patiently waiting for any old flaw
Hoping its grasp will soon be restored
Tempting me back with a voice in my head
Hoping its appetite will soon be fed

I sit and I think of the morals I've lost
The way I desired it whatever it cost
The people I've cheated, the friends I have hurt
The strangers I've robbed and treated like dirt
I did it for heroin; I did it for 'need'
It was nothing but selfish and all done for greed
I sit and weep for the person I've been
And thank God that today I am finally clean.

Catherine Hunter

A Personal Forfeit!

Often, I'm sacrificing personal happiness,
Just to give some to another!
But what a heavenly privilege to uplift and help -
Many a grieving mother
Simply wrapped in loving kindness,
It can give instant hope to a hurting soul.
There can be no finer gift, to make this priority your goal,
So refuse to look for rich rewards -
In return for any good things you do.
Then someday, when you need help most -
An angel will bring some back to you!

M Ross

For All Eternity

You look for me amongst the crowd
Yet standing here I am
You call my name as desperately
The tears you cannot dry
You wish for my compassion
Though your thoughts remain the same
That no one can you let within
A heart so full of pain
You whisper words in silence
And in prayer you only hope
There's no belief in what you say
Convinced that you can cope
If only for a moment
You would stop and ask for me
'Cause then I'd take you in my arms
For all eternity!

Jim Thomas

Little Alien

I met a little alien
Who'd come from outer space,
He wore a silver uniform
And he had a large grey face.

With no ray gun in his pocket,
I said, 'You're a fool to be unarmed.
They'll shoot you, then dissect you.'
At this point he looked alarmed.

'I come in peace,' he said to me,
'I've good news from up there.'
'My friend,' I said in sympathy,
'We're humans, we don't care.'

'How could we get on with your kind,
When we fight amongst our own?'
'Twas then the alien saw common sense
And flew his spaceship home!

Kevin Baskin

Thorns

Black thorns scratch at my heart
Its vines twisting in knots, suffocate
Bitter poison seeps through open wounds
My body lies naked, torn and beaten
My spirit swings from a noose up high
Vultures tear the flesh of my mind
The walls of my castle lay as rubble
Weeds poke through cracks like forests
Seeds of despair you sowed take root

Adrian Salamon

Poetry Now Information

We hope you have enjoyed reading this book - and that you will continue to enjoy it in the coming years.

If you like reading and writing poetry drop us a line, or give us a call, and we'll send you a free information pack.

Alternatively if you would like to order further copies of this book or any of our other titles, then please give us a call or log onto our website at
www.forwardpress.co.uk

**Poetry Now Information
Remus House
Coltsfoot Drive
Peterborough
PE2 9JX**

(01733) 898101